Charles Handy is a writer and broadcaster, known to many for his 'Thoughts for Today' on the BBC's *Today* programme. He was named as Business Columnist of the Year in 1994, and his books, including *The Empty Raincoat*, have sold over one million copies worldwide. He has been, in his time, an oil executive, a business economist, a Professor at the London Business School and Chairman of the Royal Society of Arts. He and his wife Elizabeth, a portrait photographer, live in London, Norfolk and Tuscany.

Understanding Organizations
Understanding Schools as Organizations
Understanding Voluntary Organizations
Inside Organizations
The Age of Unreason
Gods of Management
The Empty Raincoat: Making Sense of the Future
Beyond Certainty
The Hungry Spirit

THOUGHTS FOR THE DAY

Charles Handy

ARROW

Published in the United Kingdom in 1999 by
Arrow Books

1 3 5 7 9 10 8 6 4 2

First published in the United Kingdom as
Waiting for the Mountain to Move in 1991 by Hutchinson

Arrow Books Limited
Random House UK Ltd, 20 Vauxhall Bridge Road, London, SW1V 2SA

Random House Australia (Pty) Limited
20 Alfred Street, Milsons Point, Sydney, New South Wales 2061, Australia

Random House New Zealand Limited
18 Poland Road, Glenfield, Auckland 10, New Zealand

Random House South Africa (Pty) Limited
Endulini, 5a Jubilee Road, Parktown 2193, South Africa

Random House UK Limited Reg. No. 954009

A CIP catalogue record for this book is available from the British Library

Papers used by Random House UK Limited are natural, recyclable products
made from wood grown in sustainable forests. The manufacturing processes
conform to the environmental regulations of the country of origin

Typeset in Poppl-Pontifex and Copperplate Gothic
with Initials in Fine Hand Plain

Printed and bound in the United Kingdom by
The Guernsey Press Co. Ltd, Guernsey, C.I.

ISBN 0 09 940525 3

CONTENTS

ACKNOWLEDGEMENTS

E VERY WRITER needs a friendly critic, every broadcaster a producer, and every author an insightful publisher. I have been lucky enough to have had all three to help these reflections take shape.

Elizabeth, my wife, is my friendly critic. She keeps me honest and humble. 'Speak from your heart,' she tells me, 'not from your head,' and she is right, because these are meant to be reflections, not sermons.

These reflections made their first appearance as *Thoughts for the Day* on the BBC's morning programme. There, Robert Foxcroft was my first producer. I am grateful to him and to all his successors, most recently David

Coomes. They coach me down the telephone lines, proving that you can have a wonderfully productive relationship with someone you never meet.

The reflections then became a book, *Waiting for the Mountain to Move*. This book, in its turn, is a selection of the most relevant of those seventy reflections. It is my hope that it will be more companionable than its elder and larger brother. There is also an audio cassette of the book, read by me, thus returning the material to its original radio format.

My publishers, Gail Rebuck, Simon King and Paul Sidey have made it all possible – and fun. You can't ask for more. I am endlessly grateful to them and all their team.

By Way of Introduction

'WOULD YOU LIKE to do a "Thought"?' asked Robert Foxcroft one day. I knew what he meant and, because I knew, was both flattered and surprised. 'Thought' was short for 'Thought for the Day', a three-minute religious reflection slotted in between the news headlines and the weather every morning on the BBC's early morning radio programme *Today*. Robert was the producer. It was that question of Robert's which, years later, gave birth to this book of reflections or thoughts.

The god-slot, as 'Thought for the Day' was popularly known, was conventionally filled by bishops, priests and rabbis and I was none of those. But I was known to Robert who acted as producer of this one daily spot as well as being vicar of St Peter's Church in Hammersmith, London. Robert felt that I, as a rather renegade professor of business with theological affinities, might relate particularly to the many thousands of business and professional people who regularly tuned in to this programme.

'Actually,' said Robert, 'a few million people are listening, but don't get conceited, they won't have tuned in to listen to you. Half of them are in their cars and use the programme to distract them from the thought of the day ahead, the others are naked in their bath or using the radio for wallpaper sound or an alarm clock as they go about their early morning chores. Your task is to say something interesting so that they really start to listen.'

I was, as I said, flattered. The first 'Thought' was scheduled for months ahead. I had a holiday in Provence looming up and I planned to use it to polish my ideas. I came back with some sample scripts. Robert read them carefully. 'Yes,' he said, 'they're about right for length, but, well, this is supposed to be A Thought

for *the* Day, not the encapsulated wisdom of a lifetime. Ideally, it needs to relate to something that's happening in the news or in your own life, a little nugget to chew on as they go to work.' I tore them up and started again – or rather I learned not to start on them until the day before so that they really would be fresh and relevant.

Robert, sadly, died not long afterwards, to leave a huge gap in the lives of his many friends. I shall forever be grateful to him because he made me think, think about what mattered to me in life, think about my beliefs, such as they were and how they came about, think particularly about how those beliefs shed light on the countless dilemmas and worries that seemed to make up the workaday world of myself and people like me.

Three minutes, 540 words or so. It doesn't sound much, but it's the most difficult thing I ever have to do and in many ways the most rewarding – when and if it comes right. It is a great privilege to be allowed to share your personal beliefs with millions of others, whether they're listening or not, to be given three minutes with no interruptions, no questions asked, no editing. The presenters in the studio have no warning or knowledge of what I'm going to say and the rules are that they must let me say it. I sometimes wonder what would happen if I abandoned my script and started to hurl abuse at the BBC, the Prime Minister or the Queen, calling down upon them the wrath of God. Would anyone then interrupt?

Most of these reflections are slightly edited versions of those early morning 'Thoughts'. Some arose from other occasions. They spread over five years, five years which saw the end of the Cold War and the start of a Gulf War. Five years which, nearer home and the lives of most of us, saw stock markets and housing markets boom and bust, earthquakes in San Francisco and hurricanes in unusual places like southern England; but five years, too, which saw the ups and downs of life in home and office continue as they have always done, whatever happens in the big world outside.

My task, as I saw it, was to look for the meaning and the moral in those happenings, if there was one, and to put them all to the test of my beliefs. Sometimes I have thought that everyone ought to be invited to compose their own 'Thought for the Day' because of the way it forces one to think. Those reflections, therefore, are just that, my reflections on life as I see it happening around me. They carry no authority, they may well be heretical, they do not pretend to tell anyone else how to think; but if they goad or encourage anyone to do their own thinking about these things I shall be well content.

The reflections fall naturally into three sections, on the Personal, on Organizations and their workings, and on Society. The reflections reflect me. Inevitably. I have therefore added a 'personal preface' in which I try to reveal a little more of me and the way my beliefs about life and the meaning of life came to be shaped.

A PERSONAL PREFACE

IT STARTED, I suppose, with the death of my father. So many things do start with a death. It makes one wonder whom and what one's own death will spring loose.

My father was a quiet man. He had been rector of the same country parish in Kildare in Southern Ireland for forty years when he retired, aged seventy-two. He was tired by then, understandably. For the last fourteen of those years he had also been Archdeacon of the Diocese. He died two years later.

I was in Paris at a business conference when I heard that he was dying. I flew back to Ireland, but he was unconscious by the time I got there and died the next day. His funeral, like all funerals in Ireland, was arranged for the day after tomorrow, a quiet family affair, back in the country church he had served for so long.

I was very fond of my father, but disappointed in him. He had turned down big city parishes, had settled for a humdrum life in the same little backwater. His life seemed to be a series of boring meetings and visits punctuated with the unchanging rhythm of Sundays, with old Mrs Atkinson and Eddie to lunch in the rectory afterwards. As a teenager I resolved never to go to church again, once I led my own life, and never to be poor again.

And so it was that, much to the amazement of my friends and family, I became an oil executive and was posted to the Far East to be in charge of Marketing in Sarawak – a job and a country both unknown in the rectory. I had a good time in Malaysia, mostly spending money and drinking too much beer. I came back fat and rather sleek, and also engaged, to a beautiful English girl whom I had met in Kuala Lumpur.

She didn't think much of an oil executive's life or of her predestined role as an oil executive's hostess, so I switched to the newly-discovered academic world of Business Studies, going to the United States to pick up another degree and coming back to the infant London Business School. Soon I was a professor, gallivanting around to conferences, consulting, lunching, dining, on the edge of the big time. A book had been published and articles galore. We had two young children, a flat in town and a cottage in the country. More than that, I was tremendously busy, with a diary crammed with engagements. Success!

It was with these thoughts in mind that I followed the hearse down the country roads to my father's funeral; a quiet end for a quiet man, I reflected. A pity that he never really understood what I was doing. When I became a professor I remember my mother's reaction to the news was to ask if this meant that I could now spend more time with the children.

Suddenly I noticed that we seemed to have a police escort; the local police had decided unasked to clear our route for the last few miles to the church. A nice compliment to a Protestant vicar in rural Catholic Ireland, but just as well because it was hard to thread our way between the queues of cars trying to get to the little country church. The place was packed, overflowing. How had they heard? He had only died the day before yesterday and there had just been the one notice in the paper.

The choir looked odd, too. Dressed in the little-boy surplices that I remembered from Sundays long ago but with older faces. I remembered some of them. Choir boys and choir girls reassembled from all the corners of Ireland, or from England too. They had dropped everything to be there. The Archbishop too, supposed to be in hospital, and still propped on a stick, was there to say to all of us how special my father had been and how he would be missed but remembered forever by so many whose lives he had touched.

As I stood by his grave, surrounded by people he had helped to marry and whose children he had later baptized and then seen marry in his church in their

turn, as I saw the tears in the eyes of the hundreds of people who had come from everywhere to say farewell to this 'quiet' man, I turned away and began to think.

Who, I wondered, would come to my funeral with tears in their eyes? What is success and who was successful, me or my father? What is one's life for, and what is the point of our existence in this world? They are not exactly new questions. I had studied philosophy. I knew the theories. I had never applied them to myself before. Not seriously.

I went back to England. It was a long hot summer that year. I resolved to change my life and my priorities. I thought I might go to theological college, might become ordained, be a priest like my father. Luckily, I now think, the bishops whom I approached told me not to be so silly. If I wanted to serve God, as they put it, I could do it much better as a Professor of Business than in a dog-collar.

They encouraged me, actually, to apply for the post of Warden of St George's House in Windsor Castle. This is a small select study centre established by Prince

Philip and the then Dean of Windsor, Robin Woods, to be a meeting place for people of influence in the churches and in other parts of society. It ran consultations on things like Justice, The Future of Work, Power and Responsibility in our Institutions, consultations at which captains of industry, trade union leaders, head teachers, civil servants and politicians mingled and debated with bishops and chaplains and each other. It was a place of retreat and reflection for busy people in a busy world, set in a courtyard behind St George's Chapel. It became my home and my obsession for the next four years.

From one extreme to another. I thought at first that they had left out a nought when I saw my salary. They provided me with a lovely house but the cost of carpeting it was more than my first year's pay. What was all this about never being poor again, I wondered. Life has a way of going full circle, and as for never going to church again, I lived in the shadow of the great Chapel of St George and attended with relish the early morning service there in the little upstairs chapel every day of every week. 'You've been to church three times today,' my startled mother-in-law said to my wife and myself once, 'and it's only Thursday!'

But I was also in charge of the study centre and was experiencing all the problems of moving into a new institution in a new field, a world where I was not known and where I knew not their ways. It was stressful. Before long I took myself off to a psychotherapist. 'What are you seeking to achieve?' he asked me. 'I just want to make the world, in some small way, a better place,' I replied. 'Oh, I see,' he said with heavy irony, 'so now we have the three of you, Jesus Christ, the Prophet Mohammed and Professor Charles Handy!' I blushed, rebuked and embarrassed, but I got the message: here I was sitting in his consulting room, sick at heart, and talking about changing the world. There was something somewhere about taking great beams out of one's own eyes first, I recalled. I needed to be surer about myself and my beliefs if I was going to be of any use to anyone else. To put it more crisply, being is essential to doing; who I am colours what I do. Was it not Dr Johnson who said, 'Who you are sounds so loudly in my ears that I can't hear what you say.'

He said something else, my psychotherapist. I had arrived late for one session. Hampstead is a long way from Windsor and the traffic can be bad. I got there at twenty minutes past the hour instead of on the hour. At 2.50 p.m. when I had been there thirty minutes his little alarm went 'ping', signalling that the normal fifty minute consultation was up. 'Oh dear,' I said, 'I've only just got going, have you anyone else coming?'

'No,' he said.

'Well, then, can I stay on?'

'No, I'm afraid not.'

'But I've only been here thirty minutes. I got delayed by the traffic.'

'That's your problem,' he said, 'not mine.'

I went away fuming, but then I reflected that he was right. I spent my life apologizing to people for things that were nothing to do with me, like the weather, the state of our street, or the rudeness of the local shopkeeper. If people arrived late for an appointment, *I* didn't cut short

the appointment, I said, 'Oh bad luck, please don't concern yourself,' and would cheerfully change my plans for
the day because of *their* poor scheduling, taking, as it
were, their failings on my shoulders and feeling noble as
I did it. This was, I now saw, to take responsibility away
from them, to steal their choices. But was not this what
Jesus Christ was supposed to have done, taken all our
sins upon himself? No, I eventually decided, that had to
be a misrepresentation of Christianity. It is not an
escapist religion. We can't go off and do as we like and
then dump all our sins or mistakes on the deity. That's
garbage-can religion with God as the garbage can.

I was beginning to realize not only that theology
was not as straightforward as it had seemed in the days
of my youth but that it was also highly practical. I could
not get on with my life or be at peace with myself until I
had sorted out some of this stuff. Being and doing are
inseparable.

Two months later I was invited by the Dean and
Canons to preach the sermon at the Sunday morning
service in St George's Chapel. It was, I was told, the first

time that a layman had preached formally in that place since it was built in the sixteenth century. Be that as it may I was suitably overawed. I decided that it would be quite inappropriate for me to try to interpret the word of God so instead I set out to explain what I saw as the point and purpose of the study centre which sat at the end of the courtyard at the back of the Chapel. It was, I said, a place where we tried to connect people's beliefs with the problems of life and of work in today's world. If I am right, I said, the central message of Christianity is that religion is not about another life in another world but about our life in this world – God became Man, as the Bible puts it. The search for that connection between belief and action is never-ending and always changing because the world and its problems are always changing. The beliefs may remain the same but their applications will always need to be rethought by each of us each year, even each day. We are forever going to be searchers after truth.

I need not have worried too much about my sermon. I had forgotten about the verger. The verger, who is the master of ceremonies on these occasions, had never been too keen on the idea. 'Sit where you like,' he had said when I asked him about the protocol, 'and wear what you like. This has never happened before. There is no precedent.' I got the distinct impression that he hoped it would never happen again. I should not therefore have been terribly surprised when the microphones failed just after I got up to speak and did not function again that morning. The ears of the faithful were not afflicted by any possible heresies that day and I learnt, yet again, that those who control the technology will always wield great negative power, so that it is as well to have them on your side. I was pleased when the verger came up to me the next day to apologize for a 'malfunctioning of the audio system' and also to ask for a copy of my address. 'Those who heard it said that it made a lot of sense.' But that, of course, was afterwards.

The ears of the faithful may not have been harmed but I learnt a lot. It was an Irishman who said, 'How do I know what I think until I hear what I say?' and I am an Irishman. It remains the best clue to learning that I know of. The need to communicate forces you to work out what you want to say and, after that, it doesn't matter too much if anyone listens or not, because what they ought to do is to work out in their turn what they want to say. Preaching, you might say, gets in the way of learning, except for the preacher.

Over four years I listened to some six thousand people in small seminars and consultations find out what they thought when they heard what they said. Some of what they said was inspiring, some was boring, some bizarre. You couldn't always predict which mouths would say which. Two years after I left the place a businessman asked me to lunch, to thank me he said. 'What for?' I asked, over the drinks. 'Because of that weekend in Windsor some years back. I heard myself saying that the sense of responsibility that goes with ownership is so important that it shouldn't be a minority right. I went away and thought about that and decided to share the ownership of my business with my workers. The agreement was signed yesterday, hence this lunch.'

Is this anything to do with religion – I used to ask myself – with the hymns and the psalms which the choir sing so beautifully in that Chapel? I'm sure it is. I'm sure that our beliefs should, and do, infect our lives. If we try to live our lives in separate compartments, one for doing, perhaps, and one for being, why then for part of the time we are living a lie, 'the truth is not in us'. That I found and still find, is not very comfortable.

Since the day of that sermon I have been trying to bring my being and my doing closer together. In time I left Windsor. It was time to go, anyway, but I was growing increasingly uncomfortable with the need to fit into my role. It is hard for being and doing to weld into one when for part of your doing you have to act a part which is not totally 'you'. All of us, in organizations, are 'role occupants' and very few of us could claim that there is a perfect match between us and our role. That, I think, is part of the problem with organizations and part of their seduction. They force us, or allow us, depending on your viewpoint, to escape from ourselves and to play a part. It can be fun, for a while. It can be damaging in the end.

To me the only answer, I gradually realized, was to be my own master and employer. Today I am a self-employed writer and teacher. It is financially more perilous but in every other way more secure. I can't now escape from myself in my work, but these days I don't want to so much. Being and doing are closer.

It is no part of my mission to foist my beliefs on to other people. That would run counter to my philosophy of life and learning. We each have to do the searching for ourselves. Nevertheless, some clues to my beliefs are there in these reflections. My concern is only to point to what *I* see as the meaning in things and to the ultimate purpose in life in order to encourage other people to find their meaning and their purpose. The nicest comments I ever had on those broadcasts were from the man who said, 'You set me thinking for the whole of that day,' and from the woman who wrote, 'I had been bedridden for three years bemoaning my bad luck in losing both my legs. After listening, I decided that I had to do something with my life so I got up and enrolled in the local college.'

Waiting for the Mountain to Move

WHEN I GET DEPRESSED I try to think of Eric Fletcher. Eric Fletcher was a Teesider who, famously, thrust his thousand job-rejection letters under Mrs Thatcher's nose on her tour of his region and stole all her glory from her for a day. Two weeks later he got a placement with a job training scheme, learning to be a printer, armed, moreover, with an interview report which describes him as bright, capable and articulate.

Mind you, I always thought that he was under-selling himself when he described himself as 'just a labouring man', incapable of learning a new skill. Anyone who has the stamina to apply for a thousand jobs and the gumption to present them to a Prime Minister has to have *something* going for him.

I hope it works out for him, because it might mean not just a change in his living standards but in the whole way he looks at life. It was, I think, the sense of helplessness which he projected, and which had, apparently, infected his whole family, which made so many identify with him but exasperated so many others.

But I have, myself, had a glimpse of how he must have felt. My blackest times are those when I feel that my life is out of my control. Things are happening, or not happening, and I seem powerless to stop them or change them. It then gets even worse when I start to hope, yes and sometimes pray, that some outside being will intervene to put things right and *still* nothing happens.

It reminds me of Kierkegaard's story of the traveller in the hill country who came to a village only to find his road onward blocked by a mountain. So he sat and waited for the mountain to move. Years later he was still there, old now and white-haired, still waiting. Then he died, but he was long remembered in the village as a

THOUGHTS FOR THE DAY

proverb, 'the man who waited for the mountain to move'.

Kierkegaard's point is that God doesn't move mountains (nor send stock markets crashing); *we climb* mountains with God's help. Don't therefore look for Him, or His agent, outside. Look for Him inside, in *you,* and using His eyes find *new* bits of you which you never knew were there.

I go along with the fourteenth-century author of that great mystical work *The Cloud of Unknowing,* 'Swink and sweat in all that thou canst and mayest,' he says, 'for to get thee a true knowing and feeling of thyself as thou art. And then, I trow, soon after that thou wilt get thee a true knowing and feeling of God as He is.' There is, you see, more to all of us than we think there is. We *must* believe that. Swink and sweat to find yourself. It has to be worth it.

BUFFALO BILL
or Me?

WHAT'S IN A NAME? Quite a lot, seemingly. At any rate lots of us are at it, changing names that is. Companies do it, sometimes with bewildering rapidity – designing company logos is the new growth industry. Whole countries do it. People do it, particularly when they marry or unmarry. I dropped the name Charlie when I went to college and became Charles – a sign of my accelerating pomposity, my parents said then.

Changing one's name is, it seems, a self-awarded licence to be different. In fact it is interesting to note that many people these days do not change their names when they marry – a signal perhaps that they do *not*

BUFFALO BILL OR ME? 27

intend to be different. And I remember long ago going to a rather trendy workshop in America where you were invited to invent a new name before you came with a promise that no one, not even the seminar leader, would know your real one. There were two Buffalo Bills, I recall, in that group, one Marilyn Monroe and one Anon. After much agony I went as myself, ashamed at first of my lack of imagination, then proud of my integrity. What it meant however, the seminar leader told me, was that I was there under false pretences – I didn't want to find a new 'me'.

A new name however is only the start of it. The name signals a determination to be different, to have a new beginning, a rebirth even, but who then will we decide to be? Oneself, I hope. I used to tell my students not to look over their shoulders, meaning that they did not need to ape their colleagues, that they should set their *own* standards and make their *own* definitions of success.

Bishop Richard Harries, in one of his books, has a nice story about a rabbi with an unpronounceable name, Zuzya of Hannipol. '"In the coming world," said the Rabbi, "they will not ask me why were you not Moses but why were you not Zuzya?"' and as for me, I don't want to die knowing that I had only pretended to live.

So how do I know when I'm me? It's a good question for all of us – individuals, companies, political parties even. It's like beauty, I think, or being in tune. You can't define it, but you know when it's there and when it's not there. You have to trust your eye or your ear and you have, above all, to believe that there is a tune for *you,* or as St Paul put it to the cosmopolitan and fun-loving Corinthians, the yuppies of yesteryear, you must believe that the Spirit is in each and every one of us, with a different message for each but for the good of all. If you don't believe that you'll just be a sounding brass or a clashing cymbal, or today a portable fax and a personal phone.

THE WHITE
STONE

AMERICAN PRESIDENTIAL elections are strange affairs, I say to myself every four years, and remarkably long and boring affairs too. I suppose the rationale is that if you can endure a two-year-long election you can endure anything.

The curious thing about the whole of the process is the pretence that one of these two men will run the country, alone. No one runs big organizations on their own these days, let alone countries. It has to be a team affair, although of course the man, or woman, at the head has an enormous influence. One would like therefore to know how good these two people are at running teams and more important still, at picking them. It might even be sensible to elect the team and not just the leader.

Picking teams is not easy. If they are all clones or toadies of the leader they won't work. Nor will they work well if everyone is the same sort of person as everyone else. They once staged a competition in the Albert Hall between a team of company chairmen, a team of trade union leaders and a team of students. They asked them each to build a tower with Lego bricks. The chairmen came last. They all of them wanted to talk strategy which was what they were good at, not to do the actual building.

Teams need people of all sorts of types and talents. In the jargon of my world we call them shapers, finishers and evaluators and such like. St Paul, I'm glad to say, uses a richer language when he writes to the Corinthians, talking of the different gifts of the Spirit, and the need for each part of the body to make its own contribution. The point is the same, however; you need mixes of all sorts to make things work.

This may be a problem for the leader, who has to choose the team, but it's good news for the rest of us. Lots of mixes of talents and types mean lots of room for all our individual differences. To put it bluntly, there is bound to be a team out there somewhere, sometime, where our particular personality and our particular talent would help. Some find it early, some find it late, and if *you* haven't found team or talent yet, then persevere.

When I doubt that myself, like every Monday morning, I get strange comfort from a peculiar verse in the Book of Revelation. 'To anyone who prevails, the Spirit says, I will give a white stone, on which is written a new name which no one knows except he who receives it.' It is that white stone which will tell me, I believe, who I really am and what I'm really for. When I will get it I know not. That I *will* get it I am sure.

STICKING-POINTS

I'M LUCKY, I suppose. I've never really been pushed up against death. I don't know how I would behave in a hijack – I'm rather afraid that the answer might be 'shamingly'. Lucky? Well, on second thoughts, perhaps not so lucky because I've never had to work out what my sticking-points are.

Sticking-points. The Bishop used the word when he was with me and a group of managers some years back. 'What's your sticking-point?' he asked them. 'What would you not do, no matter what?' 'Murder,' they said, 'or steal or lie.' Yet, on reflection, they weren't so sure. Would you not lie to save your life on that hijacked plane – if you thought it would work? Would you lie, or at least conceal the truth, to do a better deal in business? To sell your house or trade in your car?

The Bishop's point, I think, was that all life is based on some assumption of principle. There can never be enough laws and rules and inspectors to cover everything, particularly in organizations and in business – even in families. Life would get too complicated – and too expensive.

I remember taking a group of clergy some years back to see around the Lloyds insurance building and to meet some of the agents, underwriters and brokers, and finally the Chairman himself. 'Very impressive it is,' said the clergy, 'it all seems very efficient but it must be tremendously testing morally.' The Chairman looked bemused, I remember. 'Why?' he asked. 'Well,' they said, 'everyone seems to have two or more roles, two or more conflicting loyalties, there aren't many rules or inspectors so you have to trust people to act on principle, honourably.' 'Of course,' he said. Alas, not long after events were to prove that unprincipled people can thrive in a system based mainly on principle.

It was ironic, I reflected then, that just as Lloyds had begun to make more rules and to put up some barriers between its conflicting loyalties the stock market started to dismantle its barriers in order to remain competitive. Nobody realized at the time that the so-called Big Bang was going to make Principle and People of Principle even more precious in the City.

And not just in the City. If organizations of any sort are to be left reasonably unfettered, if individuals are to be free to exercise their own initiative, then one's

personal principles and values cannot be left on the coat-stand when you walk through the office door. Principles don't belong in one box, work in another, even if it would be convenient for some of us to think that they do.

Indeed, I do know some people who seem to operate with two sets of principles – one Sunday-best for home consumption, another more, shall we say, pragmatic for downtown. They call it sensible. I call it moral schizophrenia and a recipe for breakdown both of the individual and the organization.

I don't think it's an accident that, on the whole, the most efficient organizations are the most principled ones. Trust, after all, costs much less than checking, but for trust to work you need to have principles, and sticking-points – and they only come, I believe, from a set of beliefs.

TRUST AND THE PLUMBER

COMPARED WITH all the dramas being acted out on the news these days my problems with my plumber may sound trivial. But they too may be clues to the world we live in, a barometer on the weather ahead. He's a nice chap, our plumber, and I trust him, so when I asked him to fit an outside tap on the garden wall and agreed a price I thought that that was that.

He fixed the tap all right, but instead of putting it above the gulley so that any drips would drain away he had put it three feet to the left where it would slop all over the grass. I could see why, it was easier for him to put it there and he was always one for the short cut.

When I complained he said 'Oh – it's against Water Board regulations to put a tap above a drain. Contamination you see.' It sounded a bit odd but, as I said, he's a nice chap and I trusted him.

'Don't be silly,' said my wife, 'he's having you on.' She rang the Water Board and of course he *was* talking nonsense, telling lies to get himself out of a corner.

Well, I forgave him because I wanted him to sort it out; and he did, reluctantly. But I seem to have been required to forgive an awful lot of people lately for broken promises, missed deadlines, bad work or lost money; people I trusted but who let me down.

Can it be, I wondered, as I sat, like Job, on the building site that should have been my home, that I am really expected to take books like the Bible seriously when it says that I should forgive my brother seventy times seven when he let me down every single time? The answer, I'm afraid, is 'yes' if I want him to continue to be my brother. That's not piety, that's practicality, because no relationship can survive and grow unless we are prepared to trust and to forgive when the trust goes wrong, again and again and again. No forgiveness means no relationship.

That's the bad weather which I feel coming in our society today. Trust and forgiveness are not much in evidence today because too often neither party cares whether the relationship continues or not, neither supplier nor customer, neither organization nor contractor, sometimes neither husband nor wife. Enterprise can then come to mean 'getting away with it'; prudent people will 'trust but verify', as President Reagan used to say, while careful people watch their backs and call their lawyers.

It's a sad world, I think, when we can genuinely pray 'forgive us for *not* forgiving those who sin against us'. It's a sign that trust and love and friendship have failed, have become the luxuries of life but not its basics. For myself, I will try to choose my plumbers better and *then* will persevere, trusting against the odds, forgiving if I can because, in the end, relationships matter more than perfect plumbing, and trust is cheaper than lawyers.

NOTE

Much to my surprise, my plumber was listening when this piece was broadcast. I was worried. I need not have been. He was tickled pink, as they say, to be on the air and promised to be totally trustworthy in future. Where there is trust there is hope!

BEYOND THE MARKET

I N 1938, when Chamberlain returned from Munich with his little piece of paper, T. S. Eliot wondered whether Britain was now anything more than a collection of banks and a decent interest rate. Given the attention we pay in the media to the questions of the financial world he might wonder today whether we were anything more than a rather dishevelled stock market and a slightly *indecent* interest rate.

Coming from a Business School, as I do, I am well aware of the necessity for markets of all sorts, be they for fruit and cheese in an Italian village or for stocks and shares in an electronic one. They are simply the best way that anyone has yet found of putting an acceptable price on things. But we should be careful not to push a good idea to unhealthy extremes or we may be hamstrung by our own invention. Money, after all, was made for man's convenience, not the other way round.

To tell you the truth, I find *all* the markets rather depressing these days. Like many others, I suspect. My little portfolio of shares is presumably even littler today. I don't think that there *is* a market for my house and I don't dare to find out. My pension, I suspect, is not now all it promised to be and the market for middle-aged university teachers is decidedly bleak. My net worth, as they say, is clearly on a downturn.

My net worth but not, thank God, my real worth. I mean 'thank God' quite literally because I believe that it must ultimately be by His doing that I still *know,* in my heart, that I do have real value, no matter what the markets say. When the world depresses, that thought keeps me sane. I also cannot help but notice that the old cliché really is true, the important things in life *are* free, they are outside *any* market.

The birds were singing this morning, I noticed with relief. I didn't, couldn't buy that. Nor can you or I buy friendship or the respect of friends. Or the look in the eyes of your children. My twenty-three-year-old daughter astonished her grandmother the other day by saying that her parents were parents no.longer, but her very good friends. Her grandmother snorted in disbelief but we were tickled pink. To us that is being valued and that's beyond price.

I know, too, from bitter experience, that you can't buy a clear conscience. I still have bad dreams over something I did to someone thirty years ago. No money will rid me of that memory. Only his forgiveness. I could go on. You can't buy, I hope, the love of the one by your side, nor truth, nor sincerity, nor faithfulness. That cannot be by chance. God, it is clear, does not need markets to tell Him what things are worth. Nor should we. Not for the things that *really* matter.

E VERY YEAR, it seems, the big banks decide to write off tens and hundreds of millions of pounds as provision against bad debtors; sometimes it is because some Third World countries have not repaid their loans but sometimes, recently, it has been because some big businesses which they helped to finance have regrettably collapsed. Just occasionally I wonder why it is that when the banks do this they are commanded for their prudence, but if ever I, in my small way, were to make such gross errors of judgement it would be called an unforgivable mistake. It's wonderful what you can do with words.

Words and money mattered too in the Irish rectory where I grew up. Each week my parents would prepare and exchange their personal accounts, in an attempt to keep some track of their spending. It was a weekly agony for my mother who could never remember what she had spent on what. I used to try to help. 'Why,' I

once asked, 'do you spend so much sometimes on the SPG when we are so poor?' A child of the rectory, I knew about the SPG; it was the Society for the Propagation of the Gospel in Foreign Parts, a famous missionary society. 'Hush,' said my mother, 'and never tell your father, but SPG really stands for Something, Probably Grub.'

It was my first realization that accountancy can sometimes be more of a creative art than a science. Looking back now I think that my father always knew and she knew that he knew but they both realized that 'keeping count' was a valuable discipline,.even allowing for the SPG.

Digging deeper, I came to realize that it is part of the tradition of every religion that we should have to render an account of our life at the end of that life. It would be prudent, therefore, that we should prepare for ourselves, from time to time, some interim accounts, some trial balances, showing what we have taken from life so far and what we have put back into it.

Balance sheets should balance. There should be as much on the giving side as on the getting side; and balance sheets should grow. Empty and emptying people haven't much to give. Of course, I am not talking money now. Other things are rather more important, when it comes to measuring one's *spiritual* net worth. To each of us, there are sortie special assets given, to be used not wasted. Perhaps it is time for an audit.

The difference is that if, by laziness, or error, our spiritual net worth declines in one accounting period, then, lucky us, we are not written off, there is no heavenly receivership, just the expectation that things will be noticeably better in the period ahead. I am forgiven but not released. That's tough spiritual banking, but, I think, good banking.

Marathons not Horse Races

Tʜᴇ sᴇᴀsᴏɴ of Lent should be a reminder to us to find more space for contemplation and rebalancing in our busy lives. 'Not so,' said one lady. She thought that the point of Lent was self-denial. 'Self-denial,' I said to her, 'has been the bane of this society and of its religions.'

No, I am not advocating some kind of orgy of self-indulgence, and yes, I do believe that self-control is important. What worries me is the whole set of attitudes which implies that being pleased with yourself is somehow suspect, that being different is dangerous, that cold showers are good for you, that high standards mean lots of losers, and that putting people down is the best way to make them spring up.

To put it bluntly, if we really did love our neighbours as ourselves most of our neighbours would have a pretty raw deal. Or, to put it another way, too much of our society seems to be designed to make most of us feel like losers most of the time, be it our examination system, our class system or our organizations. It's as if we were governed by the philosophy of the horse race in which only the first three count and the rest are also-rans.

You know, it's just possible that the mass marathon will come to be seen as the most important social invention of our age. In those marathons, you will have noticed, everyone who finishes gets a medal and winning means beating your own target, not the other runners. Why couldn't everything be like that? In some Japanese schools every child gets a prize, for *something,* and in the best of American firms you get awards for *trying,* not just for winning.

Does it matter? You bet it does, and I'll tell you why. When winning is so important, but so difficult, the best strategy must be to at least avoid losing. So, lower your sights, keep your head down and above all, don't try too hard. That way, if you fail you can always blame your laziness not your lack of ability and you can explain the laziness by claiming that the game wasn't worth the candle. I'm afraid that where humility is the mode, then apathy is the mood!

It's crazy, isn't it? I mean I need to be stroked, psychologically and positively, by someone for something *every day*. If I'm not, I get depressed and my energy slumps. And if me, then maybe others too. No wonder we the British do so pitifully in the economic effort stakes.

It's not only crazy, it's wrong. We are each meant to be different, aren't we? We are each given a bundle of talents, as I see it, in trust, to be used to improve our bit of creation and the lot of others. To ignore these talents in ourselves, to deny ourselves, is to spit in the face of the creator. To suppress them in others is tyranny.

So, why not love yourselves a little today and then love others. It's not soft! And if you ever want a thought for Lent – don't give something up, take something on.

THE PENDULUM PRINCIPLE

FOR FOUR YEARS I lived in the shadows of one of England's loveliest churches, the Chapel of St George in Windsor Castle, built in the same style as King's College Chapel in Cambridge and in the same period.

There were services there every morning and every evening and five of them on Sunday. I went to at least one and usually two every day, except, interestingly, on Sundays. What had happened, I wondered, to my adolescent determination never to go to church again?

I went because I wanted to, needed to, not at all because I had to. I had in my own experience stumbled across what Bruce Reed once called the oscillation theory of the Church. We live, as it were, on a pendulum swinging back and forth between activity and recreation. We need both. The pendulum must swing or the clock runs down.

Recreation however can be more than rest. Separate the word out into re-creation and it takes on a more powerful meaning, a sense of recharging combined with a touch of rebirth or newness. We should come out of the process not only refreshed but a little different.

We each need our stability zones to escape to in the hurly-burly of life. For some it may be the golf-course, for some, paradoxi-cally, the routine of the commuter trains, for others the garden or the pub. For me, for those four years, it

was the Chapel of St George, but it was, I found, a stability zone with shove!

The form of service, I discovered, had its own momentum. The words are designed to draw you in, pour balm and forgiveness over you, and then push you out into the world to 'live and to work' to the glory of God. And it worked; I went in tired or depressed and would come out with new determination and a new spring in my step.

And that was in spite of not being allowed to join in the singing, which was, I used to think, the point of going to church. In the Chapel the choir did it for you, and quite beautifully. That released me, I found, to lose myself in the music, in the beauty of the building, in the mystery of life. 'Being' there was as important as 'doing' in that act of worship. God, as so many have discovered, is in the stillness of things.

I needed this re-creation every day, but never on Sundays because Sundays contained no work. For some the Sunday or the Sabbath recharging can last the week. Some may make do with a monthly shot. I needed it daily and I wish now that I still had that chapel outside my door every morning and every evening. Chapels, however, are a luxury, and even, perhaps, an unnecessary artefact. We ought to be able to use just the beauty of the morning, the quiet of the evening, the touch of friends or the peace of silence to pull back, draw breath, take strength and push out again.

It is the pendulum which makes the clock go round so the pendulum must not get stuck, at one end or the other. It is as easy to lose oneself in the busyness of the church and of its service as it is in the busyness of life. So 'Swing, my people, Swing,' as the singer said.

Group-Think

Last week I went to stay with my mother-in-law. Now mothers-in-law aren't for staying with in the myth, but actually I greatly enjoy my time there. Not only does she ply me with excellent food and drink but I get to read her newspapers! That provides me with a very different view of Britain from the one which I normally get over breakfast. How strange to find that not everyone is arguing rationally about the Anglo-Irish agreement, economic forecasts or the latest business merger. What odd interests other people have!

The truth is that it's very good for me to be bereft of my normal newspapers. I have to start to think for

GROUP THINK

myself. No pre-packaged set of opinions on the issues of the day are there to confirm my prejudice and tell me what to say. My comfort-zone is removed. We are all quite good, I guess, at creating these comfort-zones – not just newspapers, but friends who think like us. It's what makes life predictable.

In the jargon of my profession it is called group-think, a state of affairs in which all around are of a common mind so that no one notices that the emperor is actually naked, or at least would never presume to say so. I shall always remember the fascinating research studies of the groups where all but one of the members are briefed beforehand to say that what is clearly the shorter of two lines seems to them to be the longer one, with the result that the one unbriefed member begins to doubt the evidence of his own eyes and will, in fact, usually agree with the majority!

It sounds bizarre. But it happens. I can think of too many times when I've nodded my head for the sake of a quiet life, when I've let myself be argued into agreeing to something which I know is wrong. A decent humility, you might say, or a respect for others. Too often it's just cowardice, or laziness – the comfort of group-think. Organizations are rife with group-think. They not only read the same newspapers, they wear the same clothes, tell the same jokes. They even glory in it, calling it 'shared values'. Shared values are great, of course, if the values are great.

But those shared values can also lull you into a sort of moral anaesthesia, where you find yourself agreeing too readily that the obvious way to deal with the fall in profits is to amputate a bit of the organization, that it's OK to fantasize your expenses because it's 'the unwritten law of the firm', that you must cut yourself in on the action because 'everyone expects it'. Cocooned by like-minds we can drift into a moral swamp like the man who was amazed to find himself jailed for being what he thought was just a clever businessman.

Truth actually is important, I reckon; being true to oneself, that is. Living a lie does not feel good and organizations which lie to themselves come to a distressingly predictable end. Best to remember the psalmist who reckoned heaven was for him 'who doeth the thing which is right and speaketh the truth from his heart', or to go with George Orwell who said that even if you are in a minority of one you aren't necessarily mad.

'Know yourself,' said the Greeks. 'Be yourself,' I would add. It may not be comfortable. It has to be better.

THREE-FACED
JUSTICE

'A FAIR DAY'S PAY for a fair day's work'. That seems a sensible enough philosophy for a business to adopt. A just pay policy, you might say.

Unfortunately it isn't quite as simple as that, for justice has always been one of those good words that mean different things to different people, and so it is with the word 'fair'. What seems fair to one can seem discrimination to another.

One view of justice, for instance, is that it means giving everyone what they need. That seems right and proper but so does the other definition: giving everyone what they deserve. Under the first definition those in

need are the first priority, under the second those who work hardest and best come first. It's an issue which has split politicians between left and right down the ages. Give them what they need pulls to the left. Give them what they deserve pulls to the right. There's even a third definition of justice, that it means giving everyone the same *unless* it is clear that giving someone a bit more benefits everyone; that is, giving special attention to the handicapped helps them to contribute to society, and, perhaps, giving great leaders big inducements benefits the rest of us.

What then is fair pay? Can it be right that one person be paid ten times more than another? 'Yes,' say some, 'if he produces ten times as much.' 'No,' say others, 'because no one needs ten times as much as another.' 'Yes,' say others, 'if that's what other people like him or her are getting.' It's the old justice problem again.

I can see why it seems perfectly fair to some that the chairman of a company gets a £100,000 increase when the foreman gets £270. I can also see why it will seem grotesquely unfair to others. 'Fair's fair' seems to beg an awful lot of questions. Nor can we leave it to the market. The market will tell us the going rate, which one might think would be the measure of what is deserved, one of the definitions of justice, but all markets are temporary and all are quirky or imperfect. It might be worth my while to pay the only plumber not on holiday in August an outrageous rate to mend my burst pipe, but that would not mean he deserves it. Markets, as they say, will tell you the price of anything and the value of nothing. Don't count on them for justice, that's for sure.

Justice, I think, wears different clothes in different circumstances. Robin Hood understood this – so does my entrepreneur friend who guarantees his employees a decent wage and a small share of the profits but takes for himself no wage but a large bonus when the good times come, trading security for risk. When you get it right I think you know you've got it right. Only remember that there's always another definition, another side to the coin. Or, to put it more crisply, in the words of the prophet Micah, 'Do justly, love mercy and walk humbly with your God.'

THE GREENER GRASS

THERE IS ONE very puzzling parable in the Bible, at least to me. Actually, there is more than one which perplexes but then parables are meant to be full of meanings and I can't claim to catch them all.

Well, this is the one about the farmer who hired some people to work on his land early one morning. As the day went on he hired a few more, and some right in the last hours of the day. Then when he came to pay them, he gave each of them the same amount, no matter how many hours they had worked. When the early birds grumbled at this, the farmer replied that he had paid *them* exactly what had been agreed and that if he chose to pay the same to the others that was due to the kindness of his heart and was no cause for them to complain.

When I first heard this story I felt that Jesus was condoning injustice *and* arbitrary pay policies. Then I learnt that the parable was about the generosity of God's love. But parables at their best carry personal messages and the message for me in this story is about the destructiveness of envy.

Some hold that envy is the spur to economic growth, and I guess that much of advertising is based on this belief. Dissatisfied souls try harder. It doesn't work that way with me. I want to pull down the others rather than climb up to them, just like the complaining labourers in the story, and when I can't I growl and rumble about the unfairness of life until self-righteous misery envelops me.

I feel that way when I see the tables which come out every year in the Sunday papers comparing typical British earnings. If you saw one recently, it would have had Britain's best-paid businessmen at the top with well

THE GREENER GRASS 69

over one million pounds a year, while professors and their ilk, like me, came a good two-thirds of the way down the list. Naturally I didn't linger long on those below me on the list; I looked spitefully and enviously at all those above me. Quite ruined that sunny Sunday afternoon.

Actually we don't even need the lists. Research shows that if organizations conceal their salary lists to stop people getting jealous then everybody makes their own guesses anyway about their colleagues and they always guess that the others are getting more than they really are. It's a sort of envious masochism in us and the result I have to say, is seldom new endeavours, seldom an end to any unfairness, just more unhappy people, just like the labourers in the parable.

So I have now resolved some things. I will try not to begrudge others their good luck in life but will wish them well with it. I will stop wondering about what might have been if I too had got in on those shares, if I had not sold the house five years ago, or left that job. I will not yearn for the grass on the other side of the fence which might be greener but seldom is, for I know, in my heart, that it is easier to walk down life's path if you look straight ahead and not over your shoulder at other people. It is certainly less depressing.

PICTURE-FRAMING

I ONCE STARTED a senior management course by asking the assembled managers what lay at the heart of their job. 'Taking decisions,' they said. 'Right,' I replied. 'Why don't you each come back here on Monday with your biggest decision of the week and we'll discuss it.' Next Monday the first manager said, rather shamefacedly, 'Last week was rather odd, I didn't actually take anything that could be called a big decision.' Neither it appeared had any of the others. 'An odd week, then?' I asked. No, in fact a very normal week. The truth is that leaders don't only, or even mostly, take decisions in well-run systems.

What do they do then? Well they spend a lot of time picking the people who pick the people who do make the decisions. I asked a Head once how he got the school to be the way he wanted it. 'I pick the Heads of Departments and the Heads of Houses,' he said, 'and then I wait five years.' But sometimes you don't have five years, and sometimes you find that your Heads have already been picked for you, or that you don't have an awful lot of choice. So what else do leaders do? What should the Chairman, the President, or the Prime Minister be worrying about? Reframing, I would suggest; not paintings but pictures in the mind. Good leaders are adept at reframing problems, at putting old facts into new bottles, at reconceptualizing the familiar so that new solutions leap up. Here's one example. A friend recently criticized an acquaintance of ours for bringing, as she put it, another bastard into the world. The word startled me. I hadn't heard it in its literal sense for ten years. Whoever coined the phrase 'single-parent family' had reframed the whole situation so that new behaviours, new attitudes and new laws became not only possible but obvious. There's an unsung leader there, somewhere. Do that for a whole nation or an organization and you set a sort of chemical reaction underway.

Mahatma Gandhi, to go to the other extreme, was a great reframer, turning a resistance movement from active to passive and so making it ultimately invincible. John Kennedy likewise – no great decision-maker he, but his reframing energized a nation and part of the world. I wish we could train more people to be great reframers but I fear that, even in the best of our business schools, we can only develop it a little if it's actually there. Those who have it are blessed indeed, and greatly needed.

This is the real challenge to any President, of a country or a business, to do more creative reframing for their world, to create a picture of the task which gives meaning to existence and endeavour. But it is also a challenge for all those, in politics or management, in education or in the media, who aspire to lead others, for management is just a tug-of-war when the picture has no frame, and politics a petty squabble. I sometimes think that we forget that Jesus Himself took few decisions, gave few commands, did very little. If you wrote out His CV it would read like a failure. We know now, of course, that He was reframing the picture – and changing the world. There's hope there for the rest of us; it is not our own dull CV that will be remembered but the pictures we reframed for others.

The 'They' Syndrome

'They really ought to do something about it,' said the taxi driver the other night, pointing at the traffic jammed up ahead of us. Who 'they' were or what they should do was, naturally, not specified. It was just another example of what I have come to call the 'they' syndrome – after the woman who told me that she was having to move out of her married quarters with her child because she was separating from her army husband. 'Where are you going to live then?' I asked. 'They haven't told me,' she said. 'Who are they?' I said, curious. She looked at me as if I was peculiarly

stupid. 'They haven't told me who they are, have they?'
she said witheringly.

I shouldn't be so scathing. I spent ten years in a big
company waiting patiently for them to shape my life
while *they* deplored my lack of gumption in taking no
initiatives. And I'm often wondrously tolerant of expert
authority. When the doctor told me that they knew
nothing about the cause of my virus and could not cure
it, I murmured 'thank you', hugged my pain to myself
and went away strangely reassured that 'they' were no
wiser than me!

A proper deference, you might say. Sheer escapism is
more often the truth – and it's very pervasive. Any organization will have its 'theys' who, everyone hopes, are
taking care of the future, although, when pressed, no
one is quite sure who 'they' are. It does let the rest of us
nicely off the hook; lazily, passively we wait, for someone else.

I think that a lot of it is all to do with religion, but religion tragically misunderstood. 'Almighty God,' we pray,
and Almighty He is, but that doesn't mean that He's our

general factotum, sorting everything out for us. No, the excitement of Christianity for me is its insistence that God became a Man, that God works through us, that I can't leave it to Him, that He is in fact in me. Frightening when you think about it but, actually, it's what gives life its meaning and its purpose. I would never want to think of myself as a predetermined doll, going through the motions in the hope of Nirvana at the end.

I suppose I take what's called a high view of Man, of mankind, that is. I go along with St John who said that the divine seed dwells in us, and also with Athanasius (he of the creed) who said, 'He was humanized that we might be deified.' I refuse to be what C. S. Lewis said I should be – a small dirty object in the presence of God – that's where the 'they' syndrome starts.

Take the high view and you give power to yourself, more things become possible, I find, problems turn out to conceal opportunities, blocks turn into stepping-stones – well, most of the time. It's worth a go anyway, so why not believe in yourself for a change, and stop delegating upwards. He doesn't like it, nor should 'they'!

JESUS WAS
LAME

APRIL IS THE TIME for daffodils and for grass which grows too quickly. It is also, for some of us, the month for conferences.

Oh those conferences! Shut up in an hotel with a gaggle of people, most of them strangers, stooping to peer at each other's chests as we try to read our labels. And at every conference I seem to go through the same cycle. As soon as I arrive depression deepens. Who are all those people? So imposing, so in command, intimidating almost. So glamorous, stars in their firmament. How can I compete? Yet most of them look depressingly boring, ugly even, at first sight. No way do I want to be marooned with these people.

Coward as I am, however, I don't escape. And always by the end the miracle has started to happen. The people now look different. That one who looked so imposing was after all just a shy soul hiding behind grim lips. The dumpy one in the ill-fitting suit was a bit of a genius with a lovely twist of humour. There are no ugly

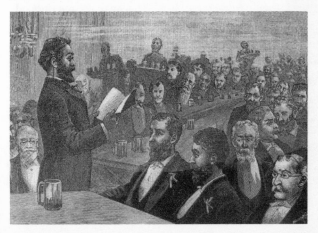

people now. Just individuals with different faces. Appearances are deceptive. Of course. But I think that there is more to it than that.

One of the nicest stories I've heard from the early Christian tradition has it that Jesus was lame. True or not I want to believe it. I would like to believe too that if He had lived a little bit longer He might also have been bald, like me. If Jesus was lame and maybe going bald, then no one mentioned it because no one noticed. Just imagine; those gospel writers, writing about the most important man who ever lived and not one of them tells us what He looked like. So if Jesus was lame and no one noticed it, why? Because of what I believe Keats meant when he wrote: 'Beauty is truth, truth beauty.' Just that. Truth is beauty, beauty truth. The truth of who you are will always shine more strongly than what you look like.

Jesus was lame and no one noticed. I find the idea very comforting as I stand in the bathroom in the morning, peering yet again at that drearily familiar face. Only be *true* and no one will notice the body I inhabit.

Only be true – true to the best in oneself, true to one's beliefs, I suppose, true to what the Roman poet Lucretius called the essence of things. It's the secret of the meaning of life, I think, this truth – and of death come to that, when real truth comes to some for the first time. Only be true. But oh, how difficult it is – even in a conference with a label on my chest telling me who I am supposed to be.

WALNUT (*Juglans regia*)

On Planting a Walnut Tree

Earlier this year I planted a walnut tree. It's a strange feeling, planting walnut trees. You know that you are never going to see that tree looking as a walnut tree should, old and gnarled and venerable and full of nuts. Some day, perhaps, your grandchildren, or more likely some stranger's grandchildren, will look up and say, 'Doesn't that walnut look great,' or will curse it when the nuts get in the way of the lawnmower. They won't thank you or curse you – they won't even think of there being a you, someone who once consciously decided to plant that tree in that place. So why was I doing it? I won't see it grown up; no one will thank me for it or remember me for it. I guess I planted it because it just seemed right and would seem right in the days after I was gone. It was, I must admit, a good feeling. I wondered why such an irrational act felt so good. It set me thinking.

I wondered first why so little of the rest of my life had this kind of perspective. I was, most of the time, more like a sower of annual flowers, looking for results this summer, or at best a planter of shrubs which have a three-year pay-off. Yet I remembered the head of a family business telling me that the great family businesses were great partly because they found it natural to 'think beyond the grave'. Their successors would be their children and their children's children. It was easier therefore to take decisions which would not pay off in their time but only in the next generation. This gave them, he said, the sense of perspective, and of long-term strategy, which so many businesses find it so hard to cultivate.

I remembered, too, a discussion about the dilemmas of modern politicians who live with the constant need to win the next election which is on average only two-and-a-bit years away, yet have, on taking office, to decide on policies which may not produce results for ten years or more. 'Who,' asked someone, 'is looking after our grandchildren when those who govern us are looking after the next election? Is it right, for instance, to build up a huge financial deficit today in order to create more jobs, which is effectively borrowing from the grandchildren to keep the grandparents comfortable?'

'Thinking beyond the grave'. It's a nice phrase. Living now so that others later can live more abundantly. Life after death, but *others'* lives after *your* death. Perhaps that is part of what Christianity is really all about.

Tough Trusting

OUR STREET, I have to tell you, is in a ferment these days. My neighbour wants to change his property, to rebuild it in fact. *He* calls the change a development and an improvement. *They* call it a disaster. The letters pouring into the planning office don't spell out, too often, quite why it would be a disaster. It is just a shame, they say, to change something that has been that way for a hundred years, even though it is falling down. Change in our street, as so often, is assumed to be change for the worse.

Yet here I am this afternoon going off to yet another management course on how to make changes happen.

To those managers it will all be heady stuff, to them change is the latest 'in' word. If you aren't an agent of change these days you are nowhere. Change for them is assumed to be change for the better. Put *them*, however, at the receiving end of someone else's changes, after a takeover for instance, and you may hear another story, for change is bad change if it isn't *your* change.

Basically, I suppose, we don't like change because we don't trust other people and because we don't trust the future. My managers need to remember that; that where there is no trust there is usually no change. I would suggest however that if we *could* trust the future *and* if we could trust ourselves then those changes would not worry us. Life after all has to change. It can't be eighty years of walking on the same spot, even if it's a nice spot. That's called marking time. Life should be a journey, and because it is always a different journey for each one of us, and always has been, it is bound to be a journey into the unknown. We should not expect the maps to be good or the guides to be reliable. Nor is it a good idea to walk it looking backwards at the past.

In fact, as I get older, I know that it is from the unexpected twists and turns in life's journey that I have learnt most and that so often what looked like deviations can turn out to be the main roads. My daughter has been struck down this year by an unexplained virus. It is difficult and depressing for her, but the other day she said to me, 'Do you know, I've never noticed the spring before.' (She is twenty-three.) 'It really is quite something. If I had not been ill I would not have looked.' Starting from there she has begun to turn this particular deviation into a time of personal investment as well as sickness.

More and more, now, I begin to glimpse what Julian of Norwich, that good lady, meant so long ago by what she called God's secret, that 'all will be well and all manner of thing will be well' even if we know not how or when. That is not wishy-washy optimism, it is the kind of *tough trust* you need if you are going to make the most of your journey. 'All manner of thing will be well' – believe that and you can take change in your stride.

THE CHOIR OF MALE CONVENIENCE

WHEN MY SON was young he had the dubious privilege of attending a choir school. It was dubious, I felt, because on top of all his schoolwork he had to do two and a half hours every day of music. It was hard work although he seemed to enjoy it.

After a bit I had cause to remark on a strange discrepancy in his end-of-term reports. Those from his form-master spoke of his generally disruptive behaviour, lack of concentration and apparent inability to learn. The choir-master, on the other hand, was full of praise for his diligence and hard work.

I spoke to the choir-master. What was his great secret, I asked. Did he beat them or threaten to lock them up? 'No,' he said, 'I do nothing, but I tell you what the difference is – in the choir they are doing proper work, with adults, and so they behave like adults."

It was a message that more teachers should learn, I thought, but I went on to wonder why it was that only in a choir school do young boys get treated as men. Then I hit on it – the only thing that grown men cannot do better than small boys is to sing in a treble voice. They have to let them in on the act, and if not small boys then soprano-voiced ladies.

Choirs are the necessary exception, it seems. Everything else has, for a long time, been organized for adult male convenience. At work, it is very convenient, is it not, that one should have a work-home-from-home that requires our presence just for those forty or fifty hours when homes need cleaning and kids need to be cared for. Inevitably it is a custom which excludes one person from that work-home and there are no prizes for guessing which that person is!

I wonder, today, how necessary it is that we should all be in the same place and all at the same time in order to get the work done. I don't wonder, actually, I know that now that most of us are assembling or processing bits of information not bits of things, it is far from essential to be all together all the time, even though we shall probably always want and need to meet our colleagues two or three times each week. You don't have to have huge office blocks full of commuters to make *that* possible. But I do wonder when we shall get round to acknowledging that a lot of that office time was always to do with male convenience. I bet that we males would not have organized things that way if it was us who had also to run a home and take the kids to school.

Ironically, I think that if we started to organize things for female convenience, with more flexibility, more control over where and when one did one's work, more personal responsibility and less minute-by-minute supervision, men might actually like it just as much as women. Well, we shall soon find out because our organizations are going to need those women more and more.

Personally, I think that organizations of male convenience have always been unnatural, in every sphere. The myth of Genesis, as I understand it, was that Adam on his own would have been a non-viable operation, or short-term at best. I still think that's true.

THE MYSTERY OF
THE UNIVERSE

I AM NO POET, but I was once asked to try my hand at poetry, to provide some of the words for a musical cantata. Here it is – the beginnings of a philosophy of religion.

There is a mystery at the heart of things.

Why don't we die?
 So much of life is worry, toil and tears
Why do we strive so busily to stay alive?
Why not just die?

THOUGHTS FOR THE DAY

What is Beauty made of?
We love the beauty in a sunset, a painting or a face
We know it's beauty when we see it, but who can say
What makes it so?

And then there's Joy
How good it is to laugh, to sing, to dance
To see the eyes of children smile - but who
Invented Joy?

There is this mystery at the heart of things

Or what of Love?
Why *should* we care for others, or put another first?
Why need the love of others to be whole ourselves?
A strange thing Love.

Whence comes our Energy?
So many strive each day to build a better world,
Putting heart and body to a stringent daily test,
Why *do* they bother?

What keeps us Good?
When the way ahead is snared with tempting traps
Like sloth and gluttony, or selfishness and greed.
Whence comes our virtue?

There is more mystery at the heart of things

Could it be chance?
We all are just a random mix of genes
Our feelings chemistry, our bodies particles in flight.
Is it all luck?

Or is there something?
Some force or reason, some point behind it all
Something that hounds us on, for each to find
A Spirit and a Truth?

Is there a mystery in the heart of things?

NOTE

The Cantata 'The Mystery of the Universe' with music by Barrie Guard, played by Andy McCullough and the Clarinet Connection, with the words narrated by Judi Dench, was published as a record by ICY Records, P. O. Box 94, SW1W 9EE in 1987.